LATE BEGINNINGS

LATE BEGINNINGS

M.A.STANIFORTH

authorHOUSE®

AuthorHouse™
1663 Liberty Drive
Bloomington, IN 47403
www.authorhouse.com
Phone: 1-800-839-8640

Published by AuthorHouse   08/20/2012

ISBN: 978-1-4772-2635-3 (sc)
ISBN: 978-1-4772-2636-0 (hc)
ISBN: 978-1-4772-2637-7 (e)

Contents

Publishing

Not knowing if a book is worth publishing or not
If it has the right credentials to make you or what
Do you invest? Or are you throwing money away
That is the question I ask myself everyday

After deciding to write and put down what I choose
I sit back thinking what have I to lose
Then the doubts creep in, what if the book is no good
What if no one likes it or if it is misunderstood

My confidence is low, I cant decide what to do
Is the book any good? I haven't a clue
To me it's a best seller, an award winning book
At least that's what I hope, with any luck

My family and friends say the book is good
Quite frankly I did expect that they would
I need an opinion one I can trust
Is it good or bad? the truth is a must

The thought of a publisher saying my book is poor
Makes my whole body cringe right to the core
The advice I require must be professional and right
To enable me to decide my book's plight

If it is acceptable and could possibly do well
Reach an acceptable standard and even sell
I would gladly invest and publish my book
But not if it doesn't deserve a second look

1 Short

It's the start of the season, it's early may
Believe it or not it's a sunny Saturday
Me and dad, set off for the ground where he plays
him with his kit bag in hand that's seen better days

At the ground stands a hut made entirely from wood
The grass is completely dry and the wicket is good
White lines are painted to create a 'boundary' line
The conditions are good and the weather is fine

My dad comes from the changing room and heads my way
He says 'we are one short, do you want to play?'
'Of course' I reply with a huge smile on my face
'I'll go and get changed' and off I race

The captains of both sides with umpires around
Throw up a coin and let it fall to the ground
Our teams fielding we have lost the toss
I hope the wrong call doesn't end in a loss

I'm on the boundary edge hidden away
Wickets are falling, I wish I could play
Wishes come true the ball is heading my way
Oops I've dropped the catch what can I say

I am totally gutted, ashamed and distraught
I got in line, was ready, did all I was taught
Can't bear to look at anyone especially Dad
What a mixture of emotions from happy to sad

Finally the fielding is done there team is all out
Not many to chase we should win no doubt
I cant stop thinking of that dropped catch
What a way to play in my fist cricket match

It's 1968 and I am the grand old age of 11 years 7 months and 19 days
The summer six week holidays are over for me in many many ways
This new term at school is more than a new teacher, class or head
But a totally new school with uniforms, prefects and single lessons instead

Just the walk to school leaves me with dread, apprehension and fear
How good or bad will school life be in the coming year
Are the horrible stories we hear all truth or lies
Do the first years get their heads flushed down the toilet and soap
poured in their eyes

All the new comers to the school gather outside of the main door
What should we all do? No one is quite sure
A prefect appears, we could tell with his badge, and leads us inside
Where he gives a speech about what a great school and wear its
colours with pride

We are then herded into the main hall where we look around in awe
And sat in rows of seats, told to keep quiet, no noise as if it was law
In front of us is a stage made of wood, containing seats and a large chair
We all know this is the time the Head will appear, this is his lair

Like a wolf he prowls, looks and glares around the hall
Looking for a weakness, the first young one to fall
He lays down the rules with his booming voice then lets us know
what he expects
Seeking discipline, perfection to make this school great whatever it takes

We learn what form we are in and which teacher will we get
Get warnings about everything and a list of rules that are set
Receive timetables of where and when lessons will take place
One sobering thought, five more years of this is what I have to face

5

Not a care in the world at five years old
Playing out in all weathers, hot or cold
Everyday is an adventure that must be explored
Giving great satisfaction which must be adored

To go from running on cobble stones and playing in back yards
To climbing trees and diving on grass, moving house has its rewards
No more grazed knees with falling in the street
Just grass stains and mud all over my feet

School holidays came and went in the blink of an eye
There was so much to do, thats the reason why
Football matches with fathers and sons
Cowboys and Indians with make believe guns

Sandwich for lunch then back out to play
No time for cooked meals too much of a delay
Important to make the most of every day light hour
Before mum calls you in for your night time shower

When your five years old and your life becomes so much fun
You haven't a care in the world when all is said and done
Its too much of a shame to have to grow up and mature
When adventure and fun is such an impressive lure

70's

To remember my youth when years roll by
Is something to cherish, says he with a sigh
A child of the fifties but a youth of the seventy
With flares all around and levi's a plenty

Ben Sherman shirts with button down collar and tag
High waisted trousers the 'Oxford Bag'
Short hair then long hair whatever the trend
The 'Mono' record player your ever present friend

The music was awesome with 'Top of the Pops' doing us proud
With groups like 'Slade', 'T Rex', 'Sweet' playing it loud
Motown Records brought 'Soul' into our lives and hearts
'Stevie Wonder' 'Diana Ross' and many more all playing their parts

The nights at the 'Youth Club' all dressed up and acting big
Trying for that first kiss, and smoking your first cig
Being clever and drinking cheap cider then being sick
Trying to act cool but end up looking like a dick

The memories of youth are still imprinted in the mind
With certain memories I would rather leave behind
All the girls I went with were loved in my own way
I can honestly say I remember them all to this day

Birth

Three in the morning and I am awoken by several shrieks
The day has arrived, we've waited nine Months and three weeks
I go into headless chicken mode, not knowing what to do
While Denise calmly phones the Hospital and talks it through

She's done this before, with Gemma ten years ago
This is my first, but not an excuse apparently though
It is the fourth of July America's special day
Hopefully this will be mine in every way

We decide to leave Gemma with my Mum and Dad
My nerves and anticipation are now becoming quite bad
Arriving at the Hospital is strange and really surreal
My emotions are so high I can't explain how I feel

On entering the ward I notice how dim and quiet everything seems
Then we are greeted by the midwife with a smile that just beams
'Come with me we will find you a nice comfy bed'
'You my man will have to do with a comfy chair instead'

After a while Denise is examined then sent for a bath
I'm told 'to help her relax' are they having a laugh
When she returns her face is all distorted with pain
Obviously, by her comments, I am to blame

As the time goes by and there is no birth to show
The Doctor decides that Cesarian section is the only way to go
After everything is prepared and everyone knows what to do
I am told I cannot be there as the staff is a skeleton crew

Denise is wheeled into an operating theatre and out of sight
The doors are closed and I feel helpless to her plight
Five minutes later my new son is born and both are well
Our son is born, 'my son and heir' his name? Brinnel

Christmas

Christmas at our house was as good as it can be
The grottos the trimmings the tiny Christmas tree
All made the excitement build, for the special day
When as every small child knows, brings Santa on his way

The socks, not stockings hanging from the wall
Mine usually had fruit, new coins and a ball
No presents were left around or under the tree
They appeared by magic in a pillowcase for me

The cries of delight of 'look he has been'
Down the chimney into the room but was never seen?
No soot from the chimney or dirty foot mark
He must have good vision it was completely dark

He drank his sherry and ate the mince pie
Then back up the chimney to his sleigh in the sky
The presents he brought are at the foot of my bed
My imagination runs wild inside my head

The tags I must keep and not throw away
I'll need them all to send thanks another day
I must not rip the paper, must take great care
Children not ripping paper, is something quite rare

Mum wants to be careful and use it next year
Is money that tight I really fear
None of this bothers me I have to say
Fifty years on and I still love Christmas Day

Dentist

Thursday morning and I'm watching the clock
A bag of nerves, it's dentist time, don't mock
That feeling in your stomach, thoughts in your head
The needle, the drill all the objects you dread

Arriving at the surgery spot on time
Ringing the bell, entering then waiting in line
Giving your name and the dentist you see
It's just a check up, what is wrong with me

In the waiting room I see anticipation all around
Everyone sits in silence not uttering a sound
The door swings open the nurse calls my name
She is quite happy, wish I felt the same

The dentist cheerfully tells me to 'pop' onto the chair
17
Then in no time at all it tilts, I pretend I don't care
He looks in my mouth and surveys the scene
I just hope its just a polish and clean

With implement in hand he completes the test
Waiting for a decision, hoping for the best
One tooth requires filling is what I need
That's as good as it possible gets I must concede

The relief of the result and delight of getting out
Has the effect of making me want to shout
The thought of a dental appointment and treatment done
Is definitely not my idea of fun

Final

Knees a trembling and hands a shaking
Sat in the dressing room with a stomach that's aching
Waiting an eternity for the referees call
For the Manager to hand out the practice balls

The schools under 11 cup final is what we are here for
With me dreaming that the opposition wont score
I am, as you guessed my school goalkeeper in fact
Only because the previous keeper, Daryl was sacked

When the match starts we attack and attack
Even my defenders and left and right back
I'm just stood watching, doing nothing, it's quite boring
We keep attacking but can't open the scoring

Theres a shot, we've scored time to jump and cheer
We are in front in the Final, is the whistle near?
We still attack and attack but can't score again
Blow that whistle put us out of our pain

Hold on, they are mounting an attack on my net
In comes the winger I'm in position and set
Suddenly he crosses the ball away to my right
Their forward, running, meets the ball while in flight

A soul destroying volley just crisp an clean
Not a better goal for them, has there ever been
The ball crashes in to the empty goal
One massive sinking feeling down to my soul

The match is drawn we decide to share the cup
They have it for six months then us worst luck
So close to winning the cup, outright on our own
Shame on all the chances we've gone and blown

Fishing

For some unknown reason, I don't know why
I stupidly decided I'd give fishing a try
Begging mum for rod, reel and line
Coming to terms with a firm decline

Second hand rod made of fibreglass and wood
A shiny black reel that fits well and good
Yards of new line packed out with string
Threading it through every individual ring

Tying on hooks, floats shot and bait
Casting out, onto water true and straight
Tightening the line the float is in view
Throwing out maggots, but only a few

Time moves on, the float remains on show
I'm wondering if this thing is ever going to go?
All day I'm just sitting watching the line
Beginning to think this is a waste of time

The boredom is too much for me to bear
Water licked from the start, I don't care
Hundreds and hundreds participate everyday
Not me anymore, not me no way

Flood

Yet another day with torrential rain
None stop pounding, no dry spots remain
Rivers swollen, bulging and flowing fast
How long will the flood defences last?

Over worked drains that the water gushes to
Cant stop the torrent rushing through
Road side kerbs becoming harder to see
As the rain keeps on pounding endlessly

The river bursts its banks to relieve it's strain
Flooding every where along Neepsend lane
The industries, shops and pubs in it's way
Are soon overrun on this grey day

Sand bags are used to try and stem the flow
Trying to persuade the deluge of another route to go
Cars are underwater traffic lights too
Some one is rescued by an emergency crew

Trees are washed by torn up by the flood
Followed by black silt and heavy mud
People are stranded all heading for a safe place
Traffic is grid locked, moving at one pace

Suddenly the weather changes and the rain slows down
The water slows, now it wont reach the town
Then as if by magic the drains put on a spurt
Leaving behind all the damage and dirt

George

George the boxer was the finest specimen of a dog
If you threw a stick he'd come back with a log
Needless to say he wasn't the cleverest, not very smart
It was the hand he was dealt with from the start

When George came to us he was only three months old
Handsome, extremely stupid, brave and bold
This loveable character bounded into our hearts
That is when all the love and loyalty starts

He had a passion for food and just being near you
Following you around no matter what your up to
He was powerful, strong but as soft as you like
But near other dogs always up for a fight

His energy was boundless when out and on the go
Never tiring, always racing to and fro
Panting away with tongue hanging from his head
To then get him home was something to dread

His passion for food was often causing him pain
Like eating wrapped chocolate, how insane
His throat became scratched causing a loss of voice
How strange it was, a bark with no noise

George's love for life was plain as can be
He was a people dog, quite obvious to see
At his best with his family all around
Sitting or laying content, not making a sound

The happiness he brought to everyone he knew
Is only exceeded by a chosen few
Who lived with him and watched him grow
Into George the Boxer we love and know

Help

At twenty three years old is this what I really need for me?
A five minute service with just ten people to see
Old fashioned parents who want to see their daughter wed
Without a care for hers or my happiness instead

With a house just bought and mortgage on my back
Needing to work and fearing the sack
The cost of a wedding no matter how small
Leaves all the payments too close to call

It would have been better to save all the cost
The new outfit etc is money all lost
There is furniture to purchase and paint to buy
This waste of money makes me want to cry

The sevice itself is to the point and brief
This to me is a great relief
A few chosen words then 'you may kiss your wife'
What a joke, together for the rest of your life

Outside we all gather to take pictures and preen
To create an album of photos seldom seen
The Mother of the bride then the Father of the bride
Others like me trying to hide

When everything is finished and we are on our way
What will be remembered of my wedding day
The weather, the outfits, or the service that was read
Or me and my expression full of dread

Holiday Coach

Every year when I broke up from school
We went away to Blackpool
From being old enough to remember
We visited even in September

The coach trip alone was a special treat
Fighting with my Sister for the window seat
She would play eye spy from a 'Blue bird' book
Shouting occasionally 'There's one there' have a look

Drinking and eating along the way
Making this a special day
Feeling tired too excited to sleep
My eyes wide open I must keep

The last leg of the journey, looking for the Tower
Some have been looking for the last half hour
Someone shouts it's over there
I didn't see it first, I don't care

Tension builds the excitement increases
Brain is on melt down, nerves are in pieces
People gather their things, and sit and wait
Muttering quite loud 'Twenty minutes late'

The coach finally stops, the driver gets out
'Everybody off' he booms with a shout
We get off the coach and wait for the cases
There are all over the shop in different places

We head away looking for the right street
Wish we'd hurry up I'm dead on my feet
Finally there's the guest house in sight
Wonder where we might be going tonight?

Hope

Not a very good day today
Our oldest cat just passed away
Eighteen years from kitten to cat
Gone in a second, that is that

An oriental looking cat with silky soft fur
Just one stroke would make her meow and purr
Loved all the attention all the time
Losing her now is a such a real crime

She was a timid kitten, very shy
Called her Hope, he says fondly with a sigh
Remembering the times when she would hide
Back of the washer she would reside

The older she got the more loving she became
Fighting with her was one big game
She had mad moments running wildly around the house
Was timid enough to be scared of a toy mouse

Always the most loving everyday and everynight
Meowing away when you come into sight
Loved the attention, the stroking, the fuss
Will be sadly missed by all of us

Five years old and full of beans
Very odd saying whatever it means
Running around without worry or care
Everything in order and correctly fair

Suddenly feel tired, sleepy all washed out
Can't raise my voice can't muster a shout
Necks all swollen, swallowing brings pain
Short of energy in bed I remain

The doctors called for we just wait
Need an examination to determine my fete
There is a knock at the door and in he walks
With his big booming voice everytime he talks

The diagnosis is not too good for me
The illness needs rest in bed I must be
Glandular fever is laying me low
Just staying in bed with no where to go

Months and months with nothing do
Eating soup and tinned Irish stew
Nothing substantial or hard to force down
Everyday spent in pyjamas and gown

The Doctors here the one with the voice
He gives me the all clear I can rejoice
I can get up quickly and move around
Even put my feet on the cold ground

Too much too soon I'm quickly washed out
'Take your time' my mother would shout
Just to be up, playing, moving around
Getting back to normal, isn't life sound

To experience the feelings of love and grief
And frown upon events in disbelief
Whatever life throws up and comes your way
Makes life a battle everyday

In everyones life there are highs and lows
The need to adapt grows and grows
From being young to being old
Learning from life and from what is told

To finally find someone who is everything to you
Who spins your head and brings love that is true
To have through thick and thin whatever it takes
Take all the good or bad that this world makes

The good times the bad times all roll into one
Sharing the pain or the pleasure in time that is gone
Together for all time in heart and mind
The one true feeling that no other can find

The ups and downs of loving someone
Is insignificant when they have gone
The hurt, the emptiness and the pain
Is left for all that still remain

Meeting

It's the last Wednesday of the Month, it's meeting time
Sat round a large table hoping all the accounts come in line
Overheads, costs, labour and wages all have to be right
Did we make money? Or are we in for a fright

Minutes from the previous meeting are issued and read
Outlining agreed budgets, targets and promises said
Preying that all you've promised has been carried out and done
Being shown up in a meeting is no fun

The production department, as usual is the first on the spot
Reporting on sales, breakdowns, sickness and injuries, the lot
The usual report of back log of work or a lack of it
And moans of poor machinery and old kit

The sales department then takes it's turn
With tales of new customers and the profits we could earn
If we could only make product cheaper the work we would gain
The same old story time again and again

Finally the accounts turn to be put on the spot is here
Is it good news? Or the news that we fear
Have we made a profit and if so what is the amount
Are the sales overwhelming? Too many to count?

With pages of figures, graphs, invoices and demands
The accounts talk of cash, not in sterling, but in 'grands'
The news is quite good and then its quite bad
Not one of the best months we have had

Operation

After days and weeks of tests, scans and multiple X rays
It's weird how life can change in a matter of days
What started as a sensation, just a feeling of slight pain
Became a major concern which nearly drove me insane

From doctor to consultant to specialist and back
No one is able to decide a form of attack
The problem seems to be a problematic throat gland
Which causes a sensation of a mouth full of sand

After months of visits, discussions and technical dross
Finally a surgeon who isn't thinking of the cost
A decision is made to take out the gland and test
A simple operation and a weeks rest

On the day of the operation after a restless night
I turn up at the hospital feeling worse for my plight
My name is called out for me to enter the ward
Where I am meted and greeted by a nurse at the door

I am taken to a bed and told to sit down
And wait for a nurse who will bring pants, socks and a gown
She appears with the said and a large green box
'Put everything in it and put on pants' gown and socks'

My blood pressure is taken it is reading slightly high
The thought of an operation, can't think why
All the other 'pre-op' tests come back fine
Then an operation consent form appears for me to sign

I'm told my operation is the fourth in the queue
Three hours to wait with nothing to do
Trying to relax and think about what is to be
And constantly worrying what the surgeon might see

The time arrives and I'm walked to the operating room
All I can muster is a feeling of doom and gloom
The anetheatist approaches with a syringe in hand
Stating 'in ten seconds you'll be out and so will the gland'

I awake to someone shouting out my name
Asking to be left alone with the soreness and pain
I am told that all went well and the gland was removed
Just have to wait for the biopsy to see what has been proved

After three hours of waiting I am allowed to get dressed
Told I can go home, I am suitably impressed
To have an operation and be in and out in a day
Everything carried out with the minimum of delay

Now a weeks wait to see what the biopsy shows
But a feeling of elation as the sand sensation goes
Deep down I know that things will now improve
Once my throat and mouth can soothe

Ton

Striding out to bat, all dressed in white
Opening the innings, a pure delight
Taking my guard from the umpires stance
Scratching out a line like some crazy dance

There is a man in white with ball in hand
Marking out a run up, marking the land
He turns and stops and looks all around
He waits for me to take my ground

The umpire is ready, he shouts out play
Finally, finally the first ball is on it's way
The ball is quite wide I am able to leave
Allowing the keeper little time to retrieve

The next ball is full and down leg side
I move quickly forward with one long stride
The ball is met by the middle of the bat
Straight for four and that is that

As time goes on and overs go past
I'm still at the crease, scoring runs at last
Partners come and go but I'm still there
Crashing fours and sixes without a care

Time is running out the overs are nearly through
I strike the ball and call for 'two'
Theres cheers and applause from those watching the game
I've scored a 'Ton' this is my moment of fame

Trip

Its here its finally arrived, that seaside trip with the working mans
club
One hour on the beach one hour for lunch the rest of the time
outside the pub
The excitement as coach after coach arrives all in a row
The apprehension of what to do and where to go

The push and the shove to get the best seats and view
The club stewards marshalling everyone and telling them what to do
All the drinks and crisps are loaded from behind the club bar
One packet and one drink each will not go very far

We are on our way the excitement can be felt all around
This feeling of visiting the seaside is quite profound
Sand, sea and sun is what we are expecting today
Even though as we set off the sky is looking grey

Nothing surely can spoil this tumultuous event
When after half an hour our spending money is spent
The rest of the time its onto the beach
Leaving the arcades behind, well out of reach

On the way home almost everyone sleeps after this annual fun
When there was plenty of sand and sea but no sun
But whatever happens we will all be back next year
Kids with crisps and pop and parents full of beer

Why

The fizz, the crackle, the bang, the roar
The war time noises that chill you to the core
The screams of fear, of panic and of pain
The sight of burning, anguish and relief of all that remain

The wounded are tended, removed and carried away
Are they the lucky ones on this infamous day?
The numbers have dwindled but plenty are still ready to fight
With nervous anticipation the enemy comes into sight

'Take cover' is the shout as a shell explodes over head
The fear recedes and anger and vengeance takes over instead
Your colleagues and mates lay dead on the crimson red ground
Lives are left broken, shattered and finished all around

We are all trained to fight and above all survive
To 'cover' our mates and help keep them alive
This war has no conscience, no shame and no rules
Just inflict as much pain and suffering on theses gallant fools

When all the fighting is over and no one is left alive
When a weapon is created again which no one will survive
Perhaps then and only then will the human race concede
That fighting and wars create suffering and pain, will no one take
the lead

Match

Standing on the Kop on the on the end called Shoreham Street
Jumping around attempting to get some warmth to my feet
Listening to the announcer naming the players on both teams
Sheffield United's home ground, Bramall Lane, is our 'theatre of dreams'

The teams come out to music and wild fanatical cheers
Not from the opposition, they just shout obscenities and sneers
The players run around going through their fitness routine
Whilst the officials get their heads together to set the scene

The toss of a coin is made by the captains of each side
To kick off or change ends, one of them must decide
The sides change ends, my team are kicking the other way
Our keeper needs to be in form, we are playing a good team today

As the game gets underway there is tension all around
We do our best to support by creating plenty of sound
The opposition are struggling to stop us we are playing well
As Football is what it is the outcome no one can tell

We attack down our right, cross the ball and in the net it goes
The noise from the supporters just grows and grows
Our centre forward, with nine on his back has struck once again
Hopefully we score another, go on and win, perfect game

After an hour and half of football there is no further score
All the players defending manfully, I can't take anymore
Will someone blow the final whistle and call it a day
The result was never in doubt anyway

Car

A white roof with body work of chrome and dark red
My very first car is a beauty it must be said
An up market mini with leather interior and loads more style
Flashing indicator, A posh grill and more glamour by a mile

It's called a Wolsley Hornet not to be confused with the Riley Elf
Can be looked at and admired but driven by no one except myself
After hours spent washing, cleaning and hoovering my new car out
Its time to take her for a drive and find out what she is about

Along busy roads, country lanes and down the high street
Cruising along and posing she never misses a beat
Visiting friends, relations and whoever I know
Finding somewhere to drive to and to make a show

The parts that are missing or broken or bulbs that are blown
Are replaced by obtaining from a scrap yard I've known
Even the minor detail, like the Wolsley light on the grill
Was replaced from the scrapyard and is probably working still

The Wolsley stayed looking well despite her long years
Rust was quite obvious but reliability brought no fears
Apart from petrol, oil, filters, insurance and such
This smart small car's running costs didn't amount to much

Then without sign or warning in just over a year
There was a sudden bang and she became hard to steer
The car went down on one side and buckled the door
The sub frame had broken under the floor

I limped the car home slowly as best as I could
Surveyed all the damage and noticed how sad she stood
Remembered how smart she looked when polished and clean
Her final resting place will be a scrapyard, how very obscene.

Broads

My first holiday away from the Blackpool hordes
Was for a week, down upon the Norfolk Broads
After exciting and hectic holidays spent on the West Coast
This will be quiet and relaxing, something to boast

A week on a boat made of wood and sleeping two
Cruising from village to village, five mile per hour will do
No grid lock roads or restricted traffic flow
Just open waterways with the odd yacht though

The boat itself is quite cramped and small
With a double bed that pulls down from the wall
The kitchen or galley is equipped with the right tools
With a small dining table and two tiny stools

The living area has a bench settee, narrow and tight
Which is uncomfortable if sitting on it all night
There is a television balanced on a shelf
Which continuously needs tuning by myself

The engine is loud as it chugs on it's way
And her paint work has seen a better day
Ideal for a beginner who has not steered a boat before
And some one who doesn't know his aft from his fore

This old boat with all it's noises and creeks
Which has been in service for years, months and weeks
Gave me a holiday with a difference that I can't explain
Water Gypsy was the grand old boats name

Its Friday the sixth of August my dear Dad's birthday
But today could be special for me in another way
Today is the day that most people detest
It is the day I will always remember my driving test

Three Months of lessons at one per week
A full, not provisional license is what I seek
I am impatiently waiting for my instructor to arrive
An extra one hour lesson before the test to survive

A blast from a horn means he's waiting outside
The time has come, no where to hide
I take my position in the driving seat
And drive for a hour, anything wrong I repeat

Arriving at the testing centre we park and go inside
After a while my name is called, my turn has finally arrived
I meet the examiner, shake hands and do as I am told
Answering questions only when asked, never being bold

The test begins and I feel that all is not well
He knows I've made mistakes, I am sure he can tell
I decide to make the most of the test, even though I wont pass
Finally the test centre is in sight, I am on the home stretch at last

After turning off the engine and answering questions on the High
Way Code
I really need to get out of the car, I've failed, just let me go
The examiner then asks 'May I have see your provisional license' to
this I ask 'why'
You have done well you've passed your test was his short and
welcome reply

As I exit the car with one excited leap and flurry
I realise I wont be driving in a hurry
My legs have turned to jelly they feel numb and light
Who said I wasn't nervous, been awake all night

Habit

At twelve years old acting big and clever
I made a mistake that will stay with me forever
To be in with the crowd and acting all big
I decided to try and smoke my first cig

Strutting my stuff and acting a part
That is when my habit began to start
At first it was for show, I wasn't smoking right
Then I started inhaling, now I was a smoker alright

In the early months when my money was tight
I was smoking maybe two or three a night
And as months went on and my spending money became more
My in take of cigarettes started to soar

My intentions from starting was to never smoke at school
Never run the risk of expulsion like an idiot or fool
But as the addiction took hold my intentions were lost
I needed a smoke whatever the cost

I smoked all through school and was never caught
Perhaps it may have been better, a good lesson taught
All through the years of money going up in smoke
I tried to stop smoking it wasn't a joke

Then finally at the age of fifty two
I decided to stop smoking and this time be true
Threw all my cigarettes and lighters away
I'm now fifty five and haven't smoked since that day

Hooray I'm fifty what can I say
I'm feeling sarcastic and old today
Fifty years have come and gone
I'll think I'll jump in the river Don

How sad is it that we celebrate
Getting old, tired and worse, irate
Aches and pains just everywhere
And the serious lack of original hair

What used to take a few minutes to do
Now can take an hour or two
Walking a distance now tires me out
Shattered at times what's it all about?

Tablets for this and drugs for that
Eat correctly don't get fat
What out for cholesterol look after your heart
Keep blood pressure down right from the start

Stop smoking, drinking, having two much to eat
Exercise properly, eat right and don't cheat
Is that all that is left in life for me
I never even wanted to be fifty

National

Hundreds of people about a mile long
Laughing and joking, voices in good song
Waiting with tickets or money in hand
The cheaper side or the grandstand?

It's all the same on Grand National day
Just to be on the course, whatever you pay
The atmosphere, the heritage the moment in time
Makes it all worth while, that standing in line

Once inside and becoming one of the crowd
It becomes a sense of achievement, feeling proud
To be at Aintree and this world famous event
Is simply priceless whatever you've spent

The early races on the card they come and go
The atmosphere is electric and starting to grow
With every race that passes time ticks by
The one and only Grand National draws nigh

It's here finally the horses are at the post
Bets are placed, hopefully, to return the most
The tape goes up they race to the first fence
The roar of the crowd, the atmosphere, intense

The further the race goes and your horse is still there
You start to think you could win, if only you dare
If only your horse can stay on it's feet
And the rider, the jockey can stay in the seat

My horse is running well it's over the last
Catching the horse in front then going past
I've won, brilliant, got watch the victory parade
And the wonderful horse that I backed 'Rag Trade'

Sixtysix

The Summer I remember the most of all
Was the time when England were the Kings of Football
What a day that was, the best of all time
Still etched in my memory and I was only nine

The flags and the bunting draped in the street
The euphoria and smiles on every one you meet
The opening games played at different grounds
Supporters from all Nations, different sights and sounds

The progression to the final is going well
How far we can get no one can tell
We survive the early rounds and get to the knock out part
This is when all the tension will start

Lose a game now and we are out on our ear
Knowing all this just adds to the fear
But we keep winning and getting through
England are doing what they have to

They are in the final, a wonderful day
The sun is out, the game gets underway
The opposition is Germany a well organised side
Who, like England wear their shirts with pride

The game itself is one of ebb and flow
The final result, no one can know
The end of ninety minutes, no one has won
Another thirty minutes and then surely it's done

England have won the final whistle is blown
This feeling of pride and joy I've never known
71

The whole Nation is celebrating, emotions run high
Remembering that summer of sixty six?, just makes me cry

Snip

Nervous, me nervous? Not me no way
Not about my minor operation today
I've had all my checks, explanations and tests
And also carried out the surgeons requests

Trying to be courageous and put on a brave face
Is just not me what ever the case
With letter in hand and appointment card signed
It's off to hospital with the ward to find

Greeted with a cheerful face and booming voice
'Come in and find a cubic to change in of your choice'
'Remove your clothes and put on the gown'
'When your ready come out and sit down'

When my name is called my blood runs cold
I am still trying to be brave and bold
It's not working I want to run away
'Is it possible to come back another day?'

I'm asked to lay on a table and try to be calm
Hopefully the surgeons good and wont cause me harm
I'm told a local anaesthetic is all I need
For the surgeon to do the deed

The thought of a vasectomy at thirty three years of age
To me is something of an obvious outrage
But looking back now that its all done
Life is better to be played without a loaded gun

Age

Whatever you think of when you start to get old
All becomes significant to what you were told
Pains and twinges are more than just a strain
It all is more serious and with more pain

What was once not serious, just a discomfort to bear
Is now life threatening to be treated with care
Visits to the doctors are more common place
For blood tests, scans and even a cardiac trace

Stop smoking, stop drinking and exercise more
In fact don't do anything you enjoyed before
The acceptance that getting old answers all your ills
And the only way to live is to take tablets and pills

The age old question is what course do you take
Do you enjoy life or take notice for your own sake
If in the end you can't enjoy what life may remain
Then listening to all the advice leaves nothing to gain

Continuing to live on no matter what life throws at us
Is a basic form of survival no matter the fuss
Keep taking the pills, keep going and persevere
I am told getting old is nothing to fear

Silverstone

Five thirty in the morning and outside it's still dark
Not a lot to be said about rising with the lark
Got to get ready and prepared and be on our way
We're driving a Ferrari at Silverstone today

We arrive in good time, redeem our tickets as told
Then wait for instructions outside in the cold
When called back inside we're ushered to a room
To watch a film and description of what we'll be doing soon

Outside we're taken out onto Silverstone's track
Ffitted for a helmet there is no turning back
Waiting quite nervously for a car to arrive
Can I do this? And will the car survive?

A bright red car arrives with an instructor inside
With a message 'drive a Ferrari with pride'
After being shown the controls and buckled in tight
We leave the pit lane garage and take the first right

The first circuit we take is sedate to say the best
As we go from bend to corner and over the crest
Second circuit gets faster as we master the track
Last lap the 'flying' lap no hanging back

With foot pressed down as far as it will go
Seated in a Ferrari laid back and low
The sense of speed sends you on an adrenalin high
And the power you feel it's as if you can fly
Down the hanger straight, gear six and top speed
Imagining I'm in a grand prix and in the lead
Over the start, finish line my laps are all done
Can anyone tell me 'have I won'

Moon

Just sat here remembering a certain day in nineteen sixty nine
When it seemed that all the world was waiting for a sign
It was the time when America was trying to conquer space
With them and Russia in a two horse race

We had seen crafts orbit the Moon and people walk in space
Seen them come back to Earth and land in an exact place
New technology and equipment upgraded for every flight
Meant landing on the Moon was a possible sight

The mission was called Lunar and the space craft was Apollo
This was number eleven with a few more to follow
Eleven would be special, the very first Moon landing
An actual Moon surface with an astronaut standing

Craft and equipment had all been individually made
New types of radio so accurate messages could be relayed
Tools for extracting dust and rocks from the Moons face
And analysis on the effects of weightlessness in space

All the television programmes were tuned into this event
And even though only twelve I regard it as time well spent
To see History in the making with my own eyes
To have a memory so deep that it never dies

The lunar craft nestled upright on the ground
The wait for an astronaut to emerge not a sound
A door opens wide and a silver figure appears
The time for the lunar walk and expectation nears

Finally the astronaut takes that famous step onto the dust
Man has walked on the Moon to see this is a must
A totally foreign entity and unexplored place
The total excitement of outer space.

One of my fondest memories, one I will never forget
Is of my first girlfriend and how we met
To save her blushes I wont mention her name
Just to mention life was never going to be the same

From being thirteen my life was all about
Trying to pull birds, playing football and hanging about
Then I met someone who I'll refer to as 'V'
Who asked if she could go out with me

She had been going out with one of my mates
But they had broken up quite quickly after a few dates
That's when I had seen her and she had seen me
I thought she was the prettiest 'Bird' I would ever see

The first time we went out, or if you like on our first date
In hind sight was poor, my fault, I took along a mate
We just hung around talking with me acting smart
Not a good way for a lasting relationship to start

The end of the night was the best part by a mile
I walked 'V' home kissed her goodbye and left with a smile
My first serious 'snog', well at least prolonged kiss
Something to remember, the feeling, the bliss

We went 'out together' on and off for quite a long time
And in some way grew up together and everything was fine
But we were young and other opportunities lay ahead
So instead of staying together we split up instead

I perhaps thought that after we had gone our separate ways
That we may meet up again and continue on from those early days
But 'V' found someone else more special who felt the same
We had both gone our separate ways, no one was to blame

Grandad 'B'

My Grandad Bacon left us when I was about two
So my memories of him are but seldom and few
I often wonder is it memory or what I was told
Or it is possible to remember things when two years old

My Grandad's house had a dining room for use everyday
With a 'Parlour' or front room only for use on Sunday
I think I was at the table, possibly on someone's knee
And my Grandad was sat on the chair next to me

He was wearing a flat cap and shirt with sleeves rolled up
And was continuously drinking tea from an extra large cup
I have a vague memory of him giving something to me
Possibly a small Banjo, a gents purse or mans jewellery

If I do remember right and this is not what I was told
I have another memory of Grandad Bacon when I was two years old
I'd behaved very well and wanted a reward
We'd all been to see 'Zoro' I demanded a sword

It was quite late and all the toy shops had closed for the night
I wanted to be like 'Zoro' and have a wonderful sword fight
We me crying and screaming my Grandad took me away
Promising to get me sword to play with that day

Up to toy shop and round to the back door we went
Knocked on it hard, then peered through the side vent
The door was opened by a slightly bewildered looking man
To get me a sword by the back door was my Grandad Bacons plan

The sword I got was fantastic, new and made my day
I used it to stab Grandad Bacon at home and on the way
Although these memories may be wrong they are true to me
At least I have something to relate to with Grandad B

Divorce

Coming from a line of long and lasting marriages is difficult to do
For breaking up and divorce is for others not you
Even if everything has failed and your marriage is dead
You feel you must stay together and make a go of it instead
If feels like you are a failure if divorce is the only way

Not to mention the let down or what your family will say
Talk it through, give it another chance is what goes through your mind
There must be some common ground, just look and you'll find

With solicitors involved and letters going here and there
You soon start to realise it's 'Dog eat Dog' nothing is fair
The relationship now comes under even more strain
And you know must decide whether there is anything left to gain

No compromise, no feelings, no hope and no way back
The conclusion is made to put life back on track
Divorce is the only way that anyone can see
A final separation is what it will be

That feeling of failure remains to this day
Even though it was right in every way
Both parties were unhappy and feelings were poor
It felt like you were scratching an open sore

The family rallied round to make things feel better
We even rejoiced receiving the Decree Final letter
But when I look at what my life is like now
I should have divorced her sooner, the 'cow'

Love

Feelings and emotions will always run high
When people get close and give love a try
The warmth, elation, happiness and joy
Affects everyone, man, woman, girl or boy

Just to care for someone who cares for you
Warms your heart right through and through
To react to a touch, smile or just a look
Is just from the pages of a romantic book

The tingling of the senses the loss of weight
The counting of the hours until your next date
The time spent grooming, making sure you're looking smart
The warmth of feeling the ticking of your heart

To have all these feelings for someone no matter who
Can be the start of an event of something true
These emotions can stand the test of time
And can be initiated with a look or a sign

Couples can stay in love for the rest of their life
Separations, no matter what, can cut like a knife
We all test ourselves, we enjoy that in love feeling
Even though the pain of separation is never healing

Award

One of the proudest moments of being a Dad
Was of an award won by my Son, how sad?
At school they had been asked to write a poem or rhyme
About going away or just having a really good time

He had chosen the subject of 'holiday'
And wrote about going to the coast for the day
All the literature was judged, sorted and read
My son won, brilliant, enough said

His poem was on buses and displayed inside
Just seeing it made me bristle with pride
The thought of his poem for all to see
Across South Yorkshire, How good can that be?

The award itself was presented by a famous local M.P.
By the world famous and honourable Roy Hattersley
A small crowd was gathered, Parents all around
To see the presentation to all these writers just found

Each age group that was judged received their award
Plus their work in a frame was their reward
We still have the work inside it's frame
Professionally printed and bearing my Sons name

Matthew

Another Grandson is born and all is well
So we decide to go away for a short spell
Car all packed and Southwards we head
For sand, sea, sun and relaxation instead

Driving comfortably, relaxed and calm
New Grandson in hospital, Daughters raised the alarm
Could be viral or worse his heart so small
Because he's so tiny it's difficult to call

Across country we head and then Northwards we go
Trying to drive calmly but not too slow
Finding the hospital, somewhere to park the car
Looking for admissions, hoping it's not far

At the desk we find what ward he is on
Just to find that he and the family had gone
Frantically searching, looking all around
No one to help us no family to be found

He is that ill he's been put in intensive care
With tubes and wires coming out of everywhere
His monitors are 'beeping' with every breath he can take
Someone must help him for heavens sake

The Doctors do tests and fluids they take
They get the results and a decision to make
A specialist is called who takes the stance
That immediate heart surgery is his only chance

The specialist is reported to be the best there can be
He is operating on a heart you can barely see
My Grandson is prepared and taken away
And we are moved to an area where we can stay

After several long hours which seemed like years
My Grandson returns to delay our fears
Everything went to plan and all went well
Now we must wait only time will tell

That was five years ago and now he is fine
Although he had a breathing aid for quite some time
He now is full of energy, often naughty and wild
In fact he behaves like what he is, a normal child

Grandad's

What I remember of Granddad Staniforth, my Dad's dad
Is a mixture of emotions some good and some bad
The little I can relate to or even recall
The size of the man, powerful and extremely tall

He was a kind gentle man and always caring
Always polite, respectful and never overbearing
Worked all his life manufacturing in steel
Never missing a day, no matter he would feel

The type of man honourable and true to his word
Quiet, very softly spoken and seldom heard
Would do things to keep the peace, for a quiet life
Move heaven and earth to look after his wife

Thinking back, I remember and I don't know why I do
For my memories of Granddad Staniforth are seldom and few
We were all going out somewhere and were catching the bus
And my Mum and Grandma Staniforth were making a fuss

Who will sit with who, were shall we sit and who's looking after who
'Send our Mark down here' was a shout 'there is room for two'
Grandad Staniforth had found a seat and was all alone
He was such a large man he filled the seat all on his own

For some reason and I don't why to this day
I wouldn't sit with him I turned around and ran away
Found my Mum and Dad and sat on their knee
But for some reason this memory has always stuck with me

I can only assume with the events of the day
I felt guilty the way I acted by running away
I sincerely hope I didn't cause ill feeling or stress
To that mild mannered man, my Granddad 'S'

Ronnie

When you manage a company which is relatively small
And you have worked there for years, too many to recall
The memories are many both good and bad
Some are very happy and some extremely sad

Unfortunately my abiding memory to this day
Is of one employee in particular who passed away
It wasn't an old employee nearing his retirement date
But one who was young with a family, that's what I hate

The employee, who was called Ronnie was a powerful man
Strong, talented, quick to learn, a part of any company's plan
He was a happy single man, a family far from his mind
Enjoyed a drink and going out, not the family kind

Then he met someone which made him alter his way
Changing his life, family imminent that's all I will say
Settling down finally to a life more content
Finding an existence to which he was meant

Then came a bomb shell, a bolt from the blue
Ronnie was taken ill, the diagnosis true
Tests had confirmed the illness he had
Was a lung tumor, spreading and extremely bad

In just over a year after treatments and pills
Ronnie passed away, giving way to his ills
Not even forty and passing away
I'll never forget this till my dying day

'Rag Day'

Who chose the cities 'Rag Parade' to be held in November
Freezing cold winds and torrential rain is what I can remember
Standing in the city centre street with coins in hand
Waiting for the University 'Floats' that follow the band

There is always a 'Fairy' a large male student at the head
Plus pyjama clad students pushing a metal bed
Rattling tins and buckets to put coins in
And strange sounding bands making an unholy din

They want your money for charities and aid
Why do they call it the 'Rag Parade'?
Coins are thrown from all in the crowd
Is this not dangerous for crying out loud?

Float after float with students in teams
Pass by, one after the other with different themes
The hours of work, commitment and thought
How can they retain whatever there taught

Quite frankly I am amazed what these people do
Student nurses, student doctors to name but two
Their criteria in life should be to study and learn
And evolve their knowledge in each University term

The 'Rag Parade' itself was a marvellous show
With itemised lists of where the money would go
Local charities close at hand and some far away
Would receive donations brought in on 'Rag day'

There is no 'Rag Parade' any more to see
It was all stopped by people more clever than me
It is a shame that future generations wont see
What the students and 'Rag Day' did for charity

Denise

Its March the tenth and it's Thursday night
And it's night out with some of the lads, alright
A few drinks around town in different pubs
Then to finish off go in to one of the clubs

In the centre of town we all eventually met
Then off on our tour of the pubs we would set
From one to another we would come and go
And all the time our group would grow

When the pubs finally close there is nothing more to do
Then off to the night club with a chosen few
With several to chose from, a decision is made
We decide to go where the best music is played

The 'Top Rank' is the name of the club where we went
And that is where the rest of the night was spent
For this particular night and event was special to me
It was the night I met Denise, my partner to be

We met on the dance floor, as if by chance
Where I was told Denise was desperate for a dance
Then after a dance and a very short chat
We went to the bar and there we sat

We met the next day to continue our chat
Liked each other immediately and that was that
We've been together since that very night
I have think I have finally found my Mrs right

Woodwork Trade

A four hour practical woodwork exam for an 'O level' grade
A must pass test if I want to get into the carpentry trade
Four years experience of learning how to cut, saw and plane
Could very soon in a matter of time be swept down the drain

The exam itself is vey secretive, time consuming and intense
With several difficult skills required and some common sense
Papers are handed around with drawings, materials and rules
And on the work bench is a series of needed tools

Time is to be spent studying how and what you need to do
Before starting to cut and carve it needs to be clear to you
The measurements need checking your marking out exact
It needs to be completely clear to you, a matter of fact

Once you have started the process, every second counts
And as the hours go by the tension increases and mounts
Now that all the work pieces have been sawn, planed or cut
Assembling is required, with joints of mortice and tenon, dovetail or
butt

All the work pieces go together and are fitting well
Will this work piece be good enough, can anybody tell?
Time is flying now the minutes are ticking by too fast
Everyone has finished I am the slowest and the last

A label is fastened to our work piece bearing our name
And after further inspection I realise that none are the same
Whose work piece is correct and who will make the grade
Or will none of use be good enough for the carpentry trade?

Bad News

A little bit of life has just faded inside of me
I had no notion of how hard and difficult this would be
Dad is in hospital, losing weight and looking very ill
Having blood transfusions, X rays and tests at will

The dim light in his eyes, the pale drawn look in his face
Has sunk his sense of humour and laughter without a trace
The conversations are broken, intermittent, short and bleak
His whole body, is frail and all his demeanour is weak

The regular scans he has, blood tests and numerous X rays
Are needed for assessment but make things worse in other ways
His body looks far too frail and the tests make him tire
But for the Doctors to make decisions that is what they require

The news that I was dreading, the word I didn't want to here
Is obviously on every ones mind but the results cant be clear
However the consultant, in his opinion, at what he has been shown
States it is cancer, not an ulcer, a large tumour has grown

I just cant imagine how Dad is feeling at this moment in time
This seems to have happened all at once, no warning or sign
He surely cant take all this earth shattering news into his head
I am feeling selfish, this is the one bit of news that fills me with dread

Mum is taking things quite good, or hiding her feelings extremely well
But after sixty two years of marriage, God, she must be hurting like hell
The emotions I am feeling are best described as unreal
I want to be alright for Dad, but want to show how I feel

The waiting for decisions by consultants, they seem to drag on
Why are things so prolonged? Where are they coming from?
Do I really want to know? Can I taken in more bad news
Do I have any say in this? Have I the right to choose?

Song

I would love to write a song, and hear it on a disc or show
And make it a memorable one that everyone wants to know
It could be a ballad, slow, which tugs at the heart
Or even a loud and lively one that rocks from the start

My own words put to music and possibly sung on stage
Played live by a singer or band that is all the rage
To have the power to make people happy to hear
The song that I have wrote being played loud and clear

To make people happy using music and word
On the face of it may sound largely absurd
But concerts I've visited and shows that I've seen
Are some of the happiest and emotional places I've been

What ever music you like from the classics to rock
Are all timeless like the face of a fingerless clock
People can associate music with events, places and time
I know to lose my love of music would be a terrible crime

To touch a world full of people by using words and a beat
And have the power to get someone dancing and out of their seat
Is something really special that can give a great sense of joy
Which is theirs for ever and no one can destroy

Sport

How is it after over a half a century of life on Earth
No one can explain to me for what it's worth
Why sport, in all it's shapes and wonderful disguises
Appeals in so many ways to people of all shapes and sizes

I personally owe my sanity to sport which helped me through
A dark side of my life, giving me a purpose, something to do
When times were at the blackest, with no end in sight
Cricket came to my rescue and gave me reason to fight

Thinking back, across all of my considerable amount of years
I have often used sport to assist me in overcoming my fears
When certain times were difficult and my life was quite sad
Just watching sport, not always playing, made things not too bad

I am continuing to live a life with sport to the fore
Even though at my time of life I don't partake anymore
It still seems to be the one of the most calming factors around
Where a somewhat quiet and calming, well being is found

I can get quite 'wound up' while watching a sport or a game
But that is a different sort of stress not really the same
'Ranting and Raving' at officials on playing fields or screen
Can be something strangely calming, if you see what I mean

For me when I was younger it was always cricket you see
Playing everyday of the week wasn't enough for me
All the anxieties that life and living brought my way
Once on the cricket pitch were forgotten for the day

Fencing

My Sister in her younger years, and youth club days
Decided to take up fencing, so strange in many ways
Not only is it a sport that was once a killing art
It teaches you, how to stab someone from the very start

Her chosen weapon of destruction was a sword called the 'Foil'
A light weight weapon, flexible that could bend and recoil
The training that was given relied on reaction and speed
And the ability to stab someone is all that you need

When my sister advanced in the standards that were needed
She entered a tournament in which she was seeded
Wanting to cheer her on and see how she would do
Dad and me went along to watch, we hadn't a clue

All dressed in white with the required protective gear
Mask on head, sword in hand, fully relaxed showing no fear
Wired up by their tunics to a strange looking machine
Which lights up and rings when there is a 'hit' not seen

The umpire, referee, judge or whatever they may be
Call the opponents to a mat, called a 'piste' you see
Their they stand waiting, crouched waiting to strike
Honestly this looks too polite to be a sword fight

The foils they twitch as they defend then attack
Everything is calm as they go forward then back
Suddenly without warning and out of the norm
My sister goes mad creating a storm

Chasing her opponent with an exaggerated attack
She fences down her enemy and forces her back
Then all at once her foil strikes again and again
The opposition is pinned to the wall and shrieks in pain

The bout is all over to the victor the spoils
Quite frankly this sport is dangerous, especially the foils
I am really glad this was a sport that didn't ring my bell
Where getting hurt is concerned I'm a coward, can you tell?

Life

I can't help wondering about this life of mine
If I had been born and lived in another time
Would I have been rich, famous and achieved success
Or would I have been much the same, I can only guess

I love watching anything historical and in the past
With personal accounts and memories that last and last
How people lived and worked to stay alive
And the relentless stories of struggle and pride

The ways in which they lived often with large families to feed
Toiling all day and night in order to fulfil their need
With no household gadgets to assist in their labour
And being too pride to ask for charity or favour
The hard times that crisis and war pour onto these folk
Is met with resilience, solidarity and often a joke
Life is so hard and everyday brings challenges all new
These people just carry on regardless, that's what they do

The suffering of different historical days and years
Through droughts, famine, plague which all create fears
Cannot be completely appreciated just by reading or word
And the thought that I would survive is stupid and absurd

But one thing to remember about the human race
If we had given in we would be lost without trace
The spirit of people across every era and time
Makes the thought of giving in a serious crime

One of the most humbling experiences I've ever had
Combined inner emotions of happy and sad
I had been asked to carry out a reading on a funeral day
For my partners Sister who had, too early, passed away

Jean was not only a Sister but to my partner a wonderful friend
The kind who was there for you, and to others you'd recommend
You wouldn't believe that for most of her life and time
She'd had serious health problems, she never showed any sign

Her illnesses began when she was only a few years old
So bad they were. they weakened her heart, she was told
And so in life when health and well being should be there
She was seeing specialists and doctors, this was totally unfair

With Jean living on the South Coast not far from the sea
We would visit for holidays, she was always a pleasure to see
She would travel around with us making our visit worthwhile
Having a laugh and a joke and always with a smile

Jean was the type that everyone loved from first sight
Doing all that she can to ensure things are just right
She liked to party, fill her life with happiness and fun
And spent hours and hours with Granddaughter and Grandson

To say she will be missed is the understatement of all time
I know she is missed daily, losing her so early was such a crime
She was a sister, a friend, a companion and shinning light
The saying 'Bad things happen to the good' could quite clearly be right

Book

Like the idiot that I am often known to be
I wanted to create something that others could see
I thought of a painting, a classical masterpiece in oil
Or a statue in iron or steel that no one could spoil

But, as everyone who knows me will tell you true
As an artist or sculptor I wouldn't have a clue
So I thought of a novel, perhaps a science fiction book
Or even one for reference showing how to cook

I have finally decided on the best way to go
And write about things that I truly know
To put down on paper some of the events gone by
And hope that some may make you laugh or cry

Thoughts of a long drawn out novel don't appeal to me
I want to create something that can be read easily
So I have decide to put all my stories down in rhyme
Short story like poems to be read any time

So finally to complete the final poem in my book
This five verse poem is all that it took
Page after page has been written with my own fair hand
To be fair and honest not all went as planned